A TRUE BOOK™

Queens and Princesses

Elizabeth I

Nel Yomtov

Children's Press®
An Imprint of Scholastic Inc.

Content Consultant
Mita Choudhury
Professor of History
Vassar College
Poughkeepsie, New York

Library of Congress Cataloging-in-Publication Data
Names: Yomtov, Nelson, author.
Title: Elizabeth I / by Nel Yomtov.
Other titles: Queen Elizabeth | True book.
Description: [First edition] | New York : Children's Press, an imprint of
   Scholastic Inc., 2020. | Series: A true book | Includes index. |
   Audience: Grades 4-6. | Summary: "The book explains the life of Queen
   Elizabeth I"-- Provided by publisher.
Identifiers: LCCN 2019031651 | ISBN 9780531131749 (library binding) | ISBN
   9780531134344 (paperback)
Subjects: LCSH: Elizabeth I, Queen of England, 1533-1603--Juvenile
   literature. | Queens--Great Britain--Biography--Juvenile literature. |
   Great Britain--History--Elizabeth, 1558-1603--Juvenile literature.
Classification: LCC DA355 .Y66 2020 | DDC 942.05/5092 [B]--dc23

All rights reserved. Published in 2020 by Children's Press, an imprint of Scholastic Inc.
Printed in North Mankato, MN, USA 113

SCHOLASTIC, CHILDREN'S PRESS, A TRUE BOOK™, and associated logos are trademarks and/or
registered trademarks of Scholastic Inc.

Scholastic Inc., 557 Broadway, New York, NY 10012

1 2 3 4 5 6 7 8 9 10 R 29 28 27 26 25 24 23 22 21 20

Book produced by 22 MEDIAWORKS, INC.
Book design by Amelia Leon / Fabia Wargin Design

Front cover: *Portrait of Elizabeth I
as a Princess,* 1546–1547
Back cover: Queen Elizabeth in procession
with her courtiers, 1600–1603

Find the Truth!

Everything you are about to read is true *except* for one of the sentences on this page.

Which one is **TRUE?**

T or F   Queen Elizabeth I had a son who became the king of England.

T or F   Queen Elizabeth wore makeup made of egg whites and other compounds.

Find the answers in this book.

Contents

Shakespeare's *The Tempest*

The **BIG** Truth

England's Golden Age

What were the major cultural achievements
of the Elizabethan Era? 36

5 The Final Years

The seal
of Queen
Elizabeth I

How did Elizabeth spend her later years as
England's leader? 38

A Special Queen

Queen Elizabeth I ruled England, Ireland, **and Wales from 1558 to 1603.** She eased religious tensions within her country and helped unify her people. Elizabeth encouraged the exploration of foreign lands. **By defeating Spain in war, she rid England of its most feared enemy.** Amazingly, Elizabeth achieved these accomplishments in a time when most people thought women were unfit to rule a nation. But, like all previous **monarchs,**

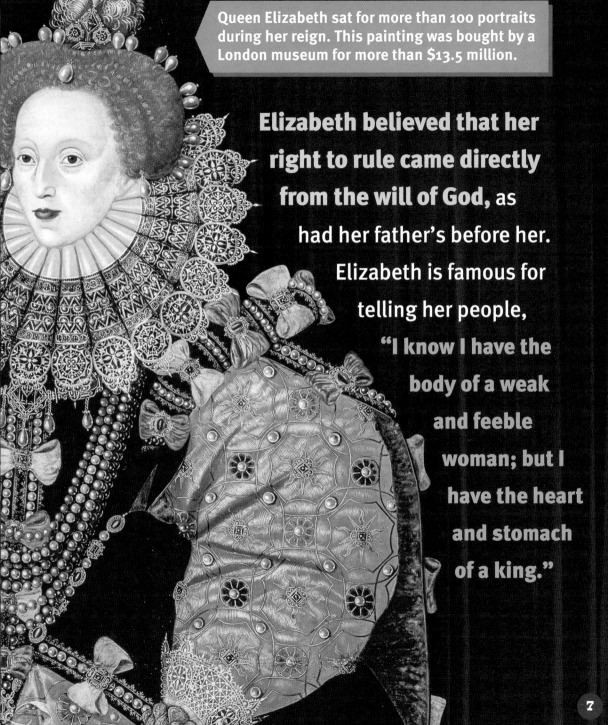

Elizabeth believed that her right to rule came directly from the will of God, as had her father's before her. Elizabeth is famous for telling her people, "I know I have the body of a weak and feeble woman; but I have the heart and stomach of a king."

Elizabeth I was neglected throughout childhood by her father, King Henry VIII.

Despite his poor treatment of her, Queen Elizabeth I modeled her rule on that of her father.

A Grand Childhood

Throughout England's long history there have been many monarchs. Only eight of these have been women. Two of England's queens—Mary I and Elizabeth I—belonged to the House of Tudor. The House of Tudor was an English royal **dynasty**, or family, that ruled England from 1485 to 1603. King Henry VII was the first English monarch from the House of Tudor. Mary and Elizabeth were the daughters of his son, King Henry VIII.

A Princess Is Born

Elizabeth Tudor was born
September 7, 1533.
King Henry VIII and
Anne Boleyn were
the parents of the
tiny baby with golden-red hair.
But Henry was disappointed.
He had hoped his child would
be a son so he would have
a male **heir** to the English
throne. Anne was Henry's second
wife. His first, Catherine of Aragon,
had borne one daughter, named Mary.
Convinced Catherine would never give birth to
a male child, Henry had decided to divorce her.

Elizabeth's cradle

A Change of Faith

Before taking a new wife, King Henry asked the pope, the head of the Catholic Church, to cancel his marriage to Catherine. At the time, Roman Catholicism was the official religion throughout Christian Europe. The pope refused Henry's request. The king angrily broke from the Catholic Church and formed the Church of England, which was Protestant. He then forced church officials to cancel his marriage to Catherine and married Anne Boleyn.

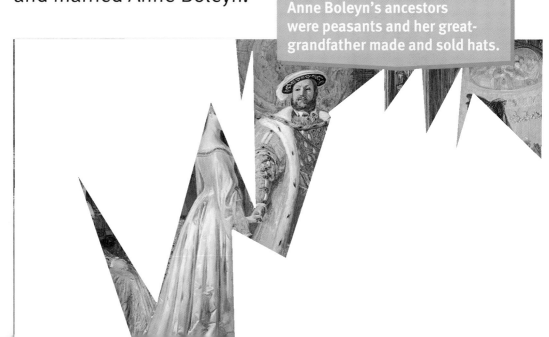

Anne Boleyn's ancestors were peasants and her great-grandfather made and sold hats.

The Young Princess

Elizabeth enjoyed a life of wealth and luxury. Anne dressed her daughter in fine clothing made of rich, colorful satins and silks. But all was not right in the royal household. When Anne failed to produce a son, King Henry accused her of **treason** and had her beheaded in 1536. Days later, Henry married his third wife, Jane Seymour. The next year, Jane gave birth to Prince Edward, but she died in childbirth.

Elizabeth's clothing was scented with lavender and spices.

Elizabeth loved to read. One account of the time claimed she "desired to look upon books as soon as the day began to break."

With a male heir to the English throne, Elizabeth's position at the royal court changed. She was now third, not second, in line to the throne, behind Edward and her sister, Mary. Instead of being called "Princess Elizabeth," the young girl was simply addressed as "Lady Elizabeth." Edward lived with his father in the royal palace in London. Elizabeth lived in the countryside at her own palace in Hatfield with its lush, magnificent gardens.

An Eager Student

Elizabeth received an excellent education. She was intelligent and eager to learn. Elizabeth took many of her lessons with Edward when she visited her father at

Elizabeth's tutor Roger Ascham developed special courses for the princess that helped her as queen.

the royal court. The young girl studied mathematics, geography, astronomy, and philosophy. She mastered penmanship and grammar. She also learned Spanish, French, Italian, Greek, and Latin. Her ability to speak different languages would later serve her well when she became queen and had to deal with foreign leaders.

More Royal Drama

King Henry VIII continued to marry. He divorced his fourth wife, Anne of Cleves, and married Catherine Howard. Henry accused Catherine of being unfaithful to him and had her beheaded also. The **instability** and violence of her father's marriages taught Elizabeth the dangers of being a wife and a queen. In 1543, Henry married his sixth and final wife, Catherine Parr. Elizabeth was 10 years old. Elizabeth grew close to Catherine and began to spend more time at the royal court.

Henry VIII was Catherine Parr's third husband. She married once more after Henry's death.

This painting portrays the family of King Henry VIII. The king is sitting in the middle, with Edward standing to his left.

Sister to the King

In 1547, King Henry VIII died. The nine-year-old prince, Edward, became the new king of England, Edward VI. During Edward's reign, Protestants rose to power in the English government. The Protestants forced Catholics to change their religious ceremonies. Edward and Elizabeth were Protestant. Mary, their sister and the next in line to the English throne, was Catholic like her mother, Catherine of Aragon. Mary was deeply troubled by the Protestant **reforms**.

Sister to the Queen

Edward VI

In 1553, Edward became ill and died. However, Edward had changed his will before his death. He did not want Mary, a devoted Catholic, to rule the country. Instead, he named Lady Jane Grey, his cousin, to become queen.

Most English people believed Mary was the rightful heir to the throne. After only nine days as monarch, Mary's supporters forced Jane Grey from power. In September 1553, Mary I was crowned queen.

Mary I

Most historians believe Mary had a lifelong hatred for her younger sister, Elizabeth.

Mary and her sister Elizabeth (in red) in church.

Peril...
and the Throne

Once more, Elizabeth's life was about to change. Queen Mary I announced that she would repair England's relations with the pope and make England Catholic again. By this time, however, most of the population was satisfied with the country's move toward Protestantism and the religious reforms made under Edward VI. Elizabeth was in a difficult situation. As a Protestant and next in line to the throne, she feared Mary might harm her.

Jailed!

Elizabeth could not openly support the Protestants who opposed Mary, nor would she **convert** to Catholicism as the queen demanded. As a result, Mary began to believe Elizabeth was a threat to her power. In 1554, the queen's spies discovered a plot that aimed to overthrow Mary and replace her with Elizabeth. Elizabeth probably knew about the plot but took no part in it. The plotters were executed, and Elizabeth was sent to prison at the Tower of London.

Elizabeth's rooms at the Tower of London were those occupied by her mother before she was beheaded.

A Fearsome Fortress

The Tower of London is a group of buildings on the northern bank of the Thames River in London. Built in the late 11th century, the Tower has served as a fortress, a royal castle, the city zoo, a prison, and a place of execution. Famous prisoners kept at the Tower include Anne Boleyn, Catherine Howard, and Elizabeth I before she became queen. Today the Tower is home to England's crown jewels. It is also a popular tourist attraction.

The value of the jewels kept at the Tower of London is more than $20 billion.

A Nation Torn Apart

Elizabeth expected to be put to death at any moment. But Mary decided to spare her sister's life. If Elizabeth were killed, Mary would have even more trouble with England's Protestants. Mary also believed that as Henry's daughter, Elizabeth was an heir, and chosen by God. Putting her to death would have meant killing someone divinely chosen to lead. In May 1554, Elizabeth was released from the Tower and sent to live in Woodstock, a small town north of London. As she was taken to her new home, people gathered in the streets to wish her well.

Mary's Reign Ends

In July 1554, Queen Mary married Prince Philip, heir to the Spanish throne and a Catholic. Mary began killing Protestants who refused to convert to Catholicism. England was torn apart as a fierce civil war erupted between the two religious groups. During this time, Queen Mary became ill. In 1558, she died of cancer. On November 17, 1558, at age 25, Elizabeth Tudor became queen of England, Ireland, and Wales.

Elizabeth is often shown wearing strands of pearls, a symbol of purity.

Queen Elizabeth's wardrobe included more than 3,000 dresses and gowns, and as many as 2,000 pairs of gloves.

Her Royal Highness, Queen Elizabeth I

Most English citizens and political leaders believed no woman was fit to rule, simply because of her gender. But Elizabeth was confident and self-assured. She was the rightful heir to the throne. Elizabeth quickly tackled the job of governing by selecting advisers she could trust. She named William Cecil as secretary of state. Cecil shared Elizabeth's desire for peace and stability within England. Robert Dudley would also become an adviser and close confidant.

A Dual Challenge

The new queen faced two major problems. England's legislature, called Parliament, urged Elizabeth to marry. Its members expected her to produce an heir to the throne and have a husband who would become England's true ruler. Some people suggested she marry Queen Mary I's widower. But Philip was Catholic and Elizabeth would not convert. Elizabeth rejected Parliament's demands and never married.

Elizabeth said, "I have already joined myself in marriage...to the kingdom of England."

On the matter of religion, Elizabeth arranged a compromise to help unite her people. The Church of England would remain Protestant, but prayer

Elizabeth had her own private chapel in most of her palaces and is believed to have prayed every day.

books and rituals designed to satisfy Catholics were added. Elizabeth's moderate actions eased tensions among her people, but they did not satisfy everyone. Many Catholics continued to practice their traditional prayers in secret. Radical Protestants, known as Puritans, still wanted Elizabeth to eliminate all traces of Catholicism in England.

A Family Affair

Mary fled Scotland in a small fishing boat, braving a dangerous journey to England.

Elizabeth had a younger cousin named Mary Stuart, known as Mary, Queen of Scots. She was the queen of Scotland and France. She was also the granddaughter of Henry VIII's oldest sister, Margaret. This relationship gave Mary a strong claim to the English throne. Mary, a Catholic queen, spent most of her life in France. When her French husband died, she returned to Scotland, a Protestant country. She married Lord Darnley, a Scotsman. The couple had a child, James, but Mary soon fell in love with another man.

Darnley murdered his rival and in turn was killed by a friend of Mary's. Angered by the distasteful events, Protestant Scots forced Mary to leave the country. Leaving behind her 13-month-old son, who became King James VI of Scotland, Mary fled to England. She hoped Elizabeth would help her regain the Scottish throne. Elizabeth did not want to risk a war with Scotland. Yet she also did not want to anger English Catholics by putting Mary in jail.

Secrets and Lies

Elizabeth allowed Mary to remain in England. However, Mary soon began plotting with Catholic supporters to overthrow Elizabeth. In 1586, Elizabeth's network of spies **intercepted** letters between Mary and her co-**conspirators**. Mary was found guilty of treason. For months, Elizabeth refused to sign her cousin's death **warrant**. She found it hard to put to death someone divinely chosen to rule. However, Mary was finally executed in 1587. Elizabeth was heartbroken.

Qu
rel
Ma
wa

New Troubles With an Old Foe

King Philip II of Spain was outraged that Elizabeth had beheaded a Catholic queen. But Philip was already furious with England. Elizabeth had encouraged English exploration. During some of these voyages, English ships attacked Spanish fleets and settlements in the **New World**. Elizabeth received a share of the treasure captured by the English sailors. By 1587, King Philip was angry enough to launch plans to invade England.

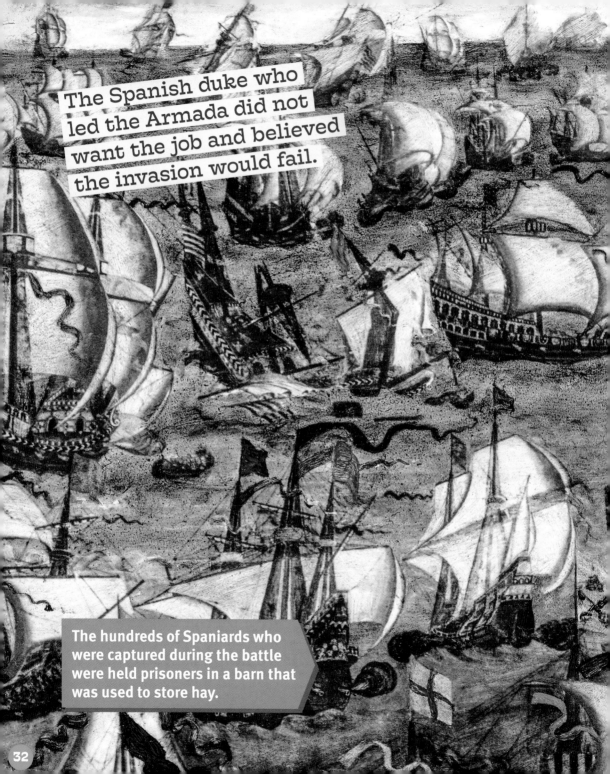

The Spanish duke who led the Armada did not want the job and believed the invasion would fail.

The hundreds of Spaniards who were captured during the battle were held prisoners in a barn that was used to store hay.

Defeating the Spanish Armada

King Philip's plan relied on the might of the Armada, a huge fleet of deadly Spanish warships. The fleet would sail up the English Channel and pick up Spanish forces stationed in the Netherlands. Then the Armada would head for England. Meanwhile, Elizabeth's spies had learned of the Spanish invasion plans. She ordered new, heavily armed ships to be built. In May 1588, after months of preparation, the Armada set sail from Spain.

Elizabeth's Shining Moment

On August 8, the Spanish fleet was anchored off the coast of France. At midnight, Elizabeth's navy set eight of its own ships on fire and sent them into the enemy formation. Fires quickly spread to the Spanish vessels. The English battered the Spaniards. In her finest hour, Elizabeth had saved her nation from invasion.

To inspire her troops, Elizabeth proclaimed, "We shall shortly have a famous victory over these enemies of my god, of my kingdom, and of my people."

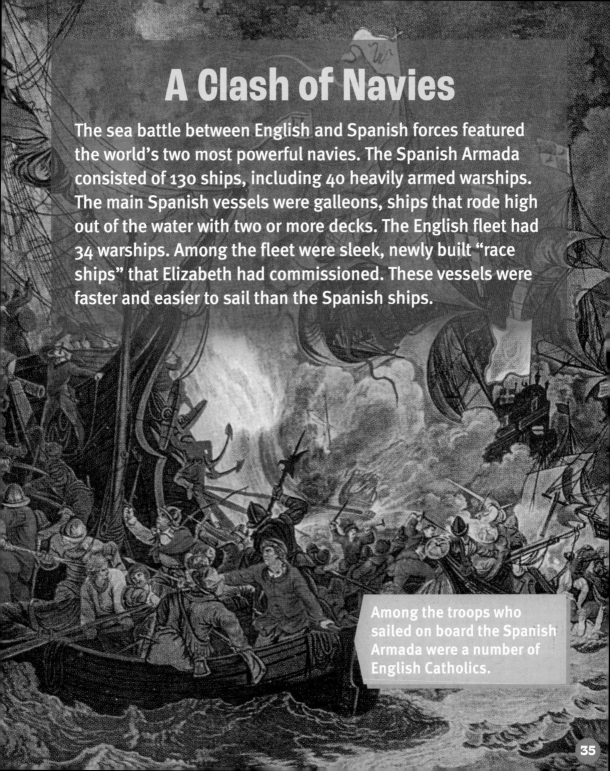

A Clash of Navies

The sea battle between English and Spanish forces featured the world's two most powerful navies. The Spanish Armada consisted of 130 ships, including 40 heavily armed warships. The main Spanish vessels were galleons, ships that rode high out of the water with two or more decks. The English fleet had 34 warships. Among the fleet were sleek, newly built "race ships" that Elizabeth had commissioned. These vessels were faster and easier to sail than the Spanish ships.

Among the troops who sailed on board the Spanish Armada were a number of English Catholics.

England's Golden Age

Historians call the reign of Queen Elizabeth the Elizabethan Era. This "golden age" in English history was one of England's greatest cultural periods, a time when exploration and various literary genres such as playwriting and poetry blossomed.

Exploration

Encouraged by Elizabeth, Sir Francis Drake sailed around the globe in search of riches for England. Sir Walter Raleigh established the colony of Virginia on America's east coast.

An old map of Raleigh's voyage to the West Indies

Playwriting

The Elizabethan Era produced the great playwright William Shakespeare. Queen Elizabeth supported the arts and the theaters in London where Shakespeare's plays were performed.

William Shakespeare

The Red Cross Knight from *The Faerie Queene*

Poetry

The Faerie Queene, written by Edmund Spenser, is an epic poem that commented on life in England. Spenser dedicated the work to Elizabeth and filled the poem with praise for the queen.

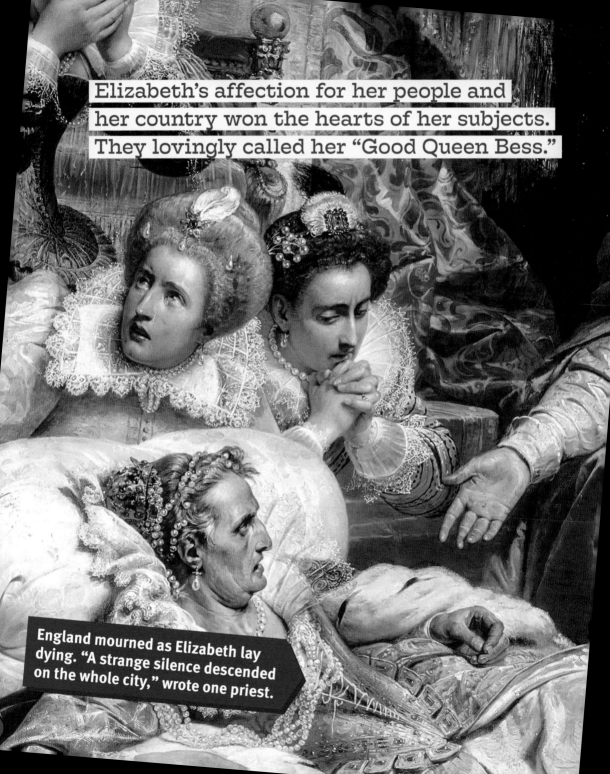

Elizabeth's affection for her people and her country won the hearts of her subjects. They lovingly called her "Good Queen Bess."

England mourned as Elizabeth lay dying. "A strange silence descended on the whole city," wrote one priest.

CHAPTER

The Final Years

During the remaining years of Elizabeth's life, England saw both prosperous and poor times. Not only did trade, literature, and foreign exploration flourish, but England was also relatively unified and at peace. At home, Elizabeth was loved and admired by her subjects. In the mid-1590s, however, a severe crop failure resulted in widespread hunger and unemployment. In 1601, a rebellion to overthrow the queen—though unsuccessful—showed that threats to the crown were still possible.

An Aging Queen

As Elizabeth aged, she wanted her people to know that she was still healthy and strong. To maintain her appearance, she followed a makeup routine common to women of nobility at the time. Elizabeth applied a mixture of egg whites, alabaster rock dust, and other compounds to her face. The makeup gave her face a pale, mask-like quality, which was a popular look in court.

Timeline: Queen Elizabeth's Life

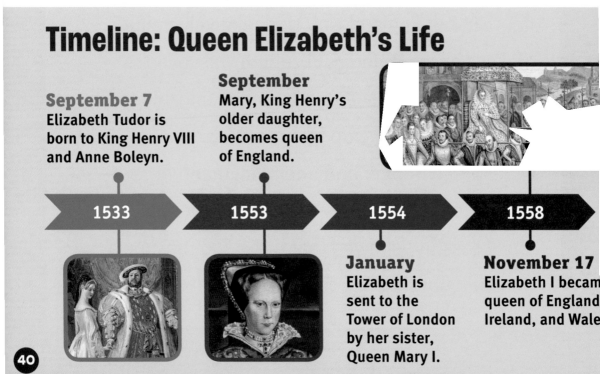

September 7
Elizabeth Tudor is born to King Henry VIII and Anne Boleyn.

September
Mary, King Henry's older daughter, becomes queen of England.

1533

1553

1554

1558

January
Elizabeth is sent to the Tower of London by her sister, Queen Mary I.

November 17
Elizabeth I becam queen of England Ireland, and Wale

In February 1603, Elizabeth fell ill. Yet she had still not decided who would follow her to the throne. On March 21, her advisers asked Elizabeth if King James VI of Scotland—the son of Mary, Queen of Scots—should be the one. Some historians believe the queen made a sign showing that she agreed. Three days later, on the morning of March 24, the 69-year-old queen died. England's golden Elizabethan Era had ended.

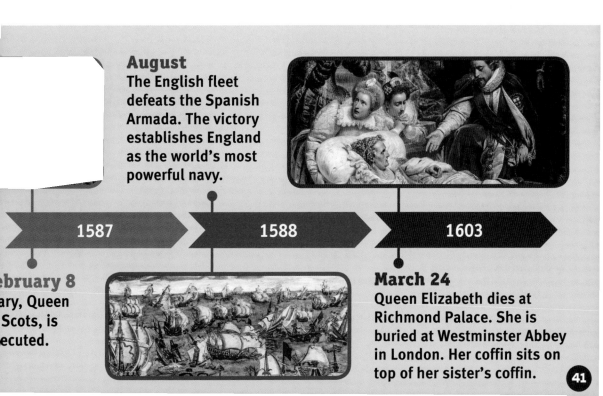

August
The English fleet defeats the Spanish Armada. The victory establishes England as the world's most powerful navy.

1587

1588

1603

ebruary 8
ary, Queen Scots, is ecuted.

March 24
Queen Elizabeth dies at Richmond Palace. She is buried at Westminster Abbey in London. Her coffin sits on top of her sister's coffin.

Elizabeth's Family Tree

Henry VIII was the king of England from 1509 to 1547.

Catherine of Aragon was the first wife of Henry VIII and the mother of Mary I. Henry divorced her in 1533 and she died three years later.

Anne Boleyn was Henry VIII's second wife and the mother of Elizabeth I. She was beheaded for treason in 1536.

Philip II became king of Spain while he was married to Mary I.

Queen Mary I was Henry VIII's elder daughter and the monarch of England from 1553 to 1558.

Queen Elizabeth I ruled England for 44 years, from 1558 to 1603. She was the only surviving child of Henry VIII and Anne Boleyn.

Jane Seymour became Henry's third wife. Jane gave birth to Edward Tudor. She died in childbirth in 1537.

Anne of Cleves, a German princess, was Henry's fourth wife. She died from cancer in 1557.

Catherine Howard became Henry's fifth wife. She was beheaded for treason in 1542.

Catherine Parr was Henry's sixth and final wife. She outlived Henry by one year, dying in childbirth in 1548.

King Edward VI ruled England from 1547 to 1553.

LEGEND

 The pink gem and dark green branches show each marriage.

 The numbers on the pink gems show the number of marriages.

The light green branches show the children of each marriage.

An orange frame indicates male.

A purple frame indicates female.

43

True Statistics

Number of royal residences owned by Elizabeth I: More than 60

Number of languages spoken by Queen Elizabeth: 10

The average number of times an upper-class person in the Elizabethan Era bathed in one month: 2

Number of sets of underwear the average English person owned in Elizabeth's time: 2 or 3

Number of hours it took for Elizabeth's ladies to dress and undress the queen: 4 hours a day

Number of kings and queens to rule under the House of Tudor: 5

Number of years Elizabeth I ruled England, Ireland, and Wales: 44

Did you find the truth?

F Queen Elizabeth I had a son who became the king of England.

T Queen Elizabeth wore makeup made of egg whites and other compounds.

Resources

Further Reading

Adams, Simon. *Elizabeth I: The Outcast Who Became England's Queen*. Washington, D.C.: National Geographic, 2005.

Greenblatt, Miriam. *Elizabeth I and Tudor England*. New York: Benchmark Books, 2002.

Hollihan, Kerrie Logan. *Elizabeth I, the People's Queen: Her Life and Times*. Chicago: Chicago Review Press, 2011.

Pratt, Mary K. *Elizabeth I: English Renaissance Queen*. Edina, MN: ABDO Publishing Company, 2012.

Stanley, Diane, and Peter Vennema. *Good Queen Bess: The Story of Elizabeth I of England*. New York: Four Winds Press, 1990.

Other Books in the Series

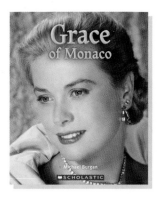
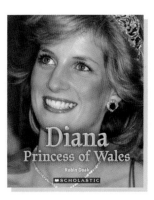

Glossary

conspirators (kuhn-SPIR-uh-turz) people who make a secret plan to do something illegal or harmful

convert (kuhn-VURT) change from one religion to another

dynasty (DYE-nuh-stee) a series of rulers belonging to the same family

heir (AIR) someone who receives someone else's money, property, or title when that person dies

instability (in-stuh-BIL-uh-tee) quality of being unbalanced, unsteady, or unpredictable

intercepted (in-tur-SEPT-id) prevented something from moving from one place to another

monarchs (MAH-nurkz) people such as kings or queens, who rule a country

New World (NOO WURLD) North and South America

reforms (ri-FORMZ) the correcting of something unsatisfactory

treason (TREE-zuhn) the crime of being disloyal to your country by spying for another country or by helping an enemy during a war

warrant (WOR-uhnt) an official piece of paper that gives someone the right to do something

Index

Page numbers in **bold** indicate illustrations.

About the Author

Nel Yomtov is an award-winning author who has written nonfiction books and graphic novels about American and world history, geography, science, mythology, careers, and mysterious, unexplained events. He has written numerous titles in Scholastic's True Books, Cornerstones of Freedom, and Calling All Innovators series. Nel lives in the New York area with his wife, Nancy, a teacher. His son, Jess, is a sports journalist.